CREATING

LONG

SENTENCES

IN ENGLISH

BOOST YOUR

COMMUNICATION SKILLS

MANIK JOSHI

Dedication

THIS BOOK IS

DEDICATED

TO THOSE

WHO REALIZE

THE POWER OF ENGLISH

AND WANT TO

LEARN IT

SINCERELY

Copyright Notice

****

IMPORTANT NOTE

This Book is Part of a Series
SERIES Name: "English Daily Use"
[A Thirty-Book Series]
BOOK Number: 08
BOOK Title: "Creating Long Sentences in English"
****

Table of Contents

Patterns For Creating Long Sentences

Creating long sentences in English is an art. You need practicing for writing and speaking long sentences. However, everyone prefer talking, reading, and listening short sentences but long sentences give strength to any language.

All of you must learn how to create long sentences in English language. Here you will learn some most popular patterns through which you will be able to form long sentences in English.

Using **–ING form of verbs** (present participle) is one of the most popular methods to make long sentences. I have given numerous examples along with their Explanation to make you understand how to use –ING form of verbs to create long sentences.

Similarly, you can use "**series** of 'similar words, phrases, thoughts, etc." for lengthening the sentence. I have also given numerous examples along with their Explanation to help you learn forming long sentence through this method.

Here, you will also learn some other methods (like using 'connecting words or phrases', parentheses, etc.) to create long sentences in English.

01 -- Using '-ING Form of Verbs' (I)

Example 01:

The ongoing drought in the state is being **described** as the country's worst in many decades, **causing** agricultural distress and **forcing** villagers to move to urban areas looking for work.

Main verb – described

-ING form of verbs – causing, forcing

Explanation:

The ongoing drought in the state is being **described** as the country's worst in many decades.

Drought is **causing** agricultural distress.

Drought is also **forcing** villagers to move to urban areas looking for work.

Example 02:

Offering huge relief to ten thousand families **belonging** to the below poverty line category in the state, minister **directed** Power Corporation Limited to waive pending domestic power bills for last 10 months.

Main verb – directed

-ING form of verbs – offering, belonging

Explanation:

Minister **directed** Power Corporation Limited to waive pending domestic power bills for last 10 months.

Minister **offered** huge relief to ten thousand families.

These Families **belongs** to the below poverty line category in the state.

Example 03:

A deadly winter storm **blanketed** a huge swath of the US, **grounding** flights, **turning** highways into the ice rinks and **knocking** out power to tens of thousands **preparing** for the New Year holiday.

Main verb – blanketed

-ING form of verbs – grounding, turning, knocking, preparing

A deadly winter storm *blanketed* a huge swath of the US.

Storm **grounded** flights.

Storm **turned** highways into the ice rinks.

Storm **knocked** out power to tens of thousands who were **preparing** for the New Year holiday.

Example 04:

From **undertaking** constructions activities when it did not have funds, never **submitting** utilization certificates for works it did, **charging** high centage than all other procuring excess expenditure and rarely **accounting** for unspent balances, the department *indulged* in financial jugglery that could put the best accountants to shame.

Main verb – _indulged_

-ING form of verbs – _undertaking, submitting, charging, accounting_

Explanation:

The department *indulged* in financial jugglery that could put the best accountants to shame.

Department **undertook** constructions activities when it did not have funds.

Department never **submitted** utilization certificates for works it did.

Department **charged** high centage than all other procuring excess expenditure.

Department rarely **accounted** for unspent balances.

Example 05:

City *continued* to reel under massive traffic jams due to water-logging as heavy rains *lashed* the city for second consecutive day, **flooding** several arterial roads and **leaving** commuters stranded for hours while **exposing** civic bodies' lack of preparedness to deal with the perennial problem.

Main verbs – _continued, lashed_

-ING form of verbs – _flooding, leaving, exposing_

Explanation:

City *continued* to reel under massive traffic jams due to water-logging.

Heavy rains *lashed* the city for second consecutive day.

Heavy rains **flooded** several arterial roads.

Heavy rains **left** commuters stranded for hours.

Heavy rains **exposed** civic bodies' lack of preparedness to deal with the perennial problem.

Example 06:

Almost all of them have *demanded* for **allowing** restaurants to remain open well past midnight as Bangalore has *become* the India's IT hub, **employing** thousands of youth not only from the state, but from across the country.

Main verbs – demanded, become

-ING form of verbs – allowing, employing

Explanation:

Almost all of them have *demanded*.

Restaurants in Bangalore should be **allowed** to remain open well past midnight.

Bangalore has *become* the India's IT hub.

It **employs** thousands of youth not only from the state, but from across the country.

Example 07:

Protestors *marched* **carrying** hammer and sickle flags & **pumping** their fists in the air.

Main verb – marched

-ING form of verbs – carrying, pumping

Explanation:

Protestors *marched*.

Protestors **carried** hammer and sickle flags.

Protestors **pumped** their fists in the air.

Example 08:

Shrugging off the looming political crisis, the Cabinet *approved* several decisions **signalling** its intent of **moving** ahead with key proposals.

Main verb – *approved*

-ING form of verbs – *shrugging, signaling, moving*

Explanation:

The Cabinet *approved* several decisions

It **shrugged** off the looming political crisis.

It **signalled** its intent.

It wanted to **move** ahead with key proposals.

Example 09:

It has *been* raining heavily since Monday night, **leaving** many roads in the tourist zone waterlogged and damaged, **including** the road connecting grassland.

Main verb – *been*

-ING form of verbs – *leaving, including*

Explanation:

It has *been* raining heavily since Monday night.

Rain has **left** many roads in the tourist zone waterlogged and damaged.

These roads **include** the road connecting grassland too.

Example 10:

The home minister *issued* a statement **regretting** the remarks ahead of the session to cool tempers.

Main verb – *issued*

-ING form of verb – *regretting*

Explanation:

The home minister *issued* a statement.

He **regretted** the remarks ahead of the session to cool tempers.

Example 11:

Indian President had *rejected* nine mercy petitions **sentencing** 14 convicts **including** a woman to death in nine months, **making** a rejection for every month of his tenure as a President.

Main <u>verb</u> – rejected

-ING <u>form</u> <u>of</u> <u>verbs</u> – sentencing, including, making

Explanation:

Indian President had *rejected* nine mercy petitions.

He had **sentenced** 14 convicts to death in nine months.

Convicts **included** a woman too.

He **made** a rejection for every month of his tenure as a President.

Example 12:

Police today *filed* charge sheet against a youth **accusing** him of having killed of a boy over two months ago and **throwing** his body outside jail.

Main <u>verb</u> – filed

-ING <u>form</u> <u>of</u> <u>verbs</u> – accusing, throwing

Explanation:

Police today *filed* charge sheet against a youth.

Police **accused** him of having killed of a boy over two months ago.

Police also accused that he had **thrown** body of a boy outside jail.

Example 13:

Commission today *issued* a show-cause notice to an officer **asking** him to submit a reply by Nov 27 **failing** which a penalty of $1000 will be deemed to have been imposed.

Main <u>verb</u> – issued

-ING <u>form</u> <u>of</u> <u>verbs</u> – asking, failing

Explanation:

Commission today *issued* a show-cause notice to an officer.

Commission **asked** the officer to submit a reply by Nov 27.

A penalty of $1000 will be deemed to have been imposed if the officer **failed** to submit a reply.

Example 14:

Acting tough against nursing homes, private hospitals, pathology labs and agencies not **disposing** of biomedical waste as per norms, City Corporation has recently **added** a new clause about their yearly renewal of license.

Main verb – added

-ING form of verbs – acting, disposing

Explanation:

City Corporation has recently **added** a new clause about their yearly renewal of license.

It has **acted** tough against nursing homes, private hospitals, pathology labs and agencies.

They were not **disposing** of biomedical waste as per norms.

Example 15:

A storm **ravaged** several districts of the state on Tuesday night, **destroying** thousands of huts and standing crops.

Main verb – ravaged

-ING form of verb – destroying

Explanation:

A storm **ravaged** several districts of the state on Tuesday night.

Thousands of huts and standing crops were **destroyed**.

Example 16:

Keeping in view the growing number of students **seeking** admission in college this academic session, the college authorities have **sought** permission to run evening classes for various graduate courses.

Main verb – sought

-ING form of verbs – keeping, seeking

Explanation:

College authorities have **sought** permission to run evening classes for various graduate courses.

College authorities **kept** in view the growing number of students who **sought** admission in college this academic session.

Example 17:

A state of emergency has been ***declared*** as raging wildfires ***spread*** in the northern part of drought-ridden state, possibly **killing** one person and **forcing** thousands to flee the flames.

Main verbs – *declared, spread*

-ING form of verbs – *killing, forcing*

Explanation:

A state of emergency has been ***declared***.

Raging wildfires ***spread*** in the northern part of drought-ridden state.

It possibly **killed** one person.

It **forced** thousands to flee the flames.

Example 18:

University ***introduced*** the online examination forms last year, **hoping** that the new software would leave lesser scope for mistakes while filling forms.

Main verb – *introduced*

-ING form of verb – *hoping*

Explanation:

University ***introduced*** the online examination forms last year.

University **hoped** that the new software would leave lesser scope for mistakes while filling forms.

Example 19:

An officer has **shot** off letters to senior officials of the companies, **seeking** an Explanation: on the issue.

Main verb – *shot*

-ING form of verb – *seeking*

Explanation:

An officer has **shot** off letters to senior officials of the companies.

He/she has **sought** an Explanation: on the issue.

Example 20:
The police *remained* tight-lipped, **saying** that investigations were on.
Main verb – remained
-ING form of verb – saying
Explanation:
The police *remained* tight-lipped.
The police **said** that investigations were on.

Example 21:
PM has *warned* party members from spreading communal hatred, **acknowledging** that provocative comments made by his party colleagues were "uncalled for" and **declaring** that constitutional guarantees of religious freedom and non-discrimination were "non-negotiable".
Main verb – warned
-ING form of verbs – acknowledging, declaring
Explanation:
PM has *warned* party members from spreading communal hatred.
PM has **acknowledged** that provocative comments made by his party colleagues were "uncalled for".
He also **declared** that constitutional guarantees of religious freedom and non-discrimination were "non-negotiable".

Example 22:
As many as 12 leading institutes of the country had *prepared* a detailed atlas **identifying** the vulnerable regions in the Himalayan ranges that could have acted as a ready reckon for the district administration in **handing** landslide-prone regions of the country.
Main verb – prepared
-ING form of verb – identifying, handing
Explanation:

As many as 12 leading institutes of the country had ***prepared*** a detailed atlas.

Atlas had **identified** the vulnerable regions in the Himalayan ranges.

These regions could have acted as a ready reckon for the district administration.

Administration could have **handled** landslide-prone regions of the country.

Example 23:

Government ***appointed*** four judges, **taking** to 12 the number of justices restored.

Main verb – appointed

-ING form of verb – taking

Explanation:

Government ***appointed*** four judges.

It **took** to 12 the number of justices restored.

Example 24:

He on his part ***sought*** to do damage control, **saying** his words had been distorted but he was ready to express regret if he had hurt the sentiments of people.

Main verb – sought

-ING form of verb – saying

Explanation:

He on his part ***sought*** to do damage control.

He **said** his words had been distorted.

He also said that he was ready to express regret if he had hurt the sentiments of people.

Example 25:

Government ***presented*** a white paper on black money in Parliament **spelling** out a strategy to curb generation of illicit money.

Main verb – presented

-ING form of verb – spelling

Explanation:

Government **presented** a white paper on black money in Parliament.

Government spelled out a strategy to curb generation of illicit money.

Example 26:

The northeast region cannot be **considered** par with other states of India **owing** to its geographical factors.

Main verb – considered

-ING form of verb – owing

Explanation:

The northeast region cannot be **considered** par with other states of India. It **owes** to its geographical factors.

Example 27:

The family **sat** at a corner table, **chatting** and **enjoying** the food.

Main verb – sat

-ING form of verbs – chatting, enjoying

Explanation:

The family **sat** at a corner table.

The family **chatted** and **enjoyed** the food.

Example 28:

He **accused** her of massive irregularities and corruption worth several millions **including** recruitment of her relatives in several posts in violation of recruitment norms and **giving** building constructions work to contractors without a proper auction.

Main verb – accused

-ING form of verbs – including, giving

Explanation:

He **accused** her of massive irregularities and corruption worth several millions.

Accusation **included** recruitment of her relatives in several posts in violation of recruitment norms.

According to accusation, she **gave** building constructions work to contractors without a proper auction too.

Example 29:

Second hand of goddess of wealth was *shown* open and **pointing** downward **showering** wealth and **reinforcing** the message of sharing.

Main verb – *shown*

-ING form of verbs – *pointing, showering, reinforcing*

Explanation:

Second hand of goddess of wealth was *shown* open.

It **pointed** downward.

It **showered** wealth.

It also **reinforced** the message of sharing.

Example 30:

She had **expressed** her inability to respond to the notice **claiming** that she was unwell and hospitalized.

Main verb – *expressed*

-ING form of verb – *claiming*

Explanation:

She had **expressed** her inability to respond to the notice.

She had **claimed** that she was unwell and hospitalized.

Example 31:

Officials **were** in the schools from the morning prayers to the lunch break, **monitoring** the quality of education imparted, **getting** to know the students' problems and **searching** for solutions for the same.

Main verb – *were*

-ING form of verb – *monitoring, getting, searching*

Explanation:

Officials **were** in the schools from the morning prayers to the lunch break.

They were **monitoring** the quality of education imparted.

They were **getting** to know the students' problems.

They were also **searching** for solutions of the problems.

Example 32:

Clamping down on unfair business practices in the aviation section, Competition commission **slapped** penalties on three carriers for cartelization in fixing fuel surcharge for transporting cargo.

Main verb – slapped

-ING form of verb – clamping

Explanation:

Competition commission **clamped** down on unfair business practices in the aviation section.

It **slapped** penalties on three carriers for cartelization in fixing fuel surcharge for transporting cargo.

Example 33:

He **parried** queries on whether he would join a political party, **saying** he will be standing wherever the interests of state are served.

Main verb – parried

-ING form of verb – saying

Explanation:

He **parried** queries on whether he would join a political party.

He **said** he will be standing wherever the interests of state are served.

Example 34:

The Armed Forces Flag Day is celebrated with great enthusiasm, **offering** a tribute to the martyred who protect the nation.

Main verb – celebrated

-ING form of verb – offering

Explanation:

The Armed Forces Flag Day is **celebrated** with great enthusiasm
It is celebrated to **offer** a tribute to the martyred who protect the nation.

ADDITIONAL EXAMPLES:

The residents were *requested* to fill up forms, **pledging** to donate any organ or whole body after death.

People *opposed* the release of gangster **citing** threat of serious law and order problem.

Tigers *attack* and *catch* dogs by throat **leaving** no chance for them to bark or raise an alarm.

Heavy rains accompanied by strong winds *battered* coastal areas **affecting** normal life at several palaces and **claiming** many lives under the influence of cyclone.

02 -- Using '-ING Form of Verbs' (II)

In the following examples –ING form of verbs have been used to show 'First Event' in the sentence.

Example 01:

The rare action has been *taken* by speaker **following** repeated disruptions in the house, the immediate provocation **being** the incidents of April 24 which saw opposition members **storming** the well **shouting** slogans without **paying** heed to the chair.

Main verb – taken
-ING form of verb – following, being, storming, shouting, paying

Explanation:

First Event – There **were** repeated disruptions in the house.

The incidents of April 24 **was** the immediate provocation.

Opposition members **stormed** the well.

They were **shouting** slogans.

They were not **paying** heed to the chair.

Second Event -- The rare action has been *taken* by speaker.

Example 02:

Police **drew** up the chain of sequence **leading** to the killing of renowned artist.

Main verb – drew
-ING form of verb – leading

Explanation:

First Event -- Something **led** to the killing of renowned artist.

Second Event – Police *drew* up the chain of sequence.

Example 03:

The local police had on Friday morning *arrested* the cousin brother of the accused **thinking** that he was the offender.

Main verb – arrested

-ING form of verb – thinking

Explanation:

First Event – The local police **thought** that the cousin brother of the accused was the offender.

Second Event – Police had on Friday morning *arrested* the cousin brother of the accused.

Example 04:

The woman *survived*, **bruising** and **injuring** her hands and feet.

Main verb – survived

-ING form of verb – bruising, injuring

Explanation:

First Event – The woman **bruised** her hands and feet.

The woman also **injured** her hands and feet.

Second Event – However, The woman *survived*.

Example 05:

Two policemen were *suspended* after video footage aired by TV channels *showed* them **joining** a mob in **beating** up an offender and **dragging** him on the street with one of his legs tied to a motorcycle.

Main verb – suspended, showed

-ING form of verb – joining, beating, dragging

Explanation:

First Event – Two Policemen **joined** a mob.

Mob was **beating** up an offender.

Policemen **dragged** him on the street.

One of his legs was tied to a motorcycle.

Second Event – Policemen were *suspended* after video footage aired by TV channels *showed* them.

Example 06:

Minister *landed* the government in severe embarrassment ***after*** a video of him purportedly **telling** state government officials that they could steal a little provide they were working hard ***became*** public.

Main verb – landed, became

-ING form of verb – telling

Explanation:

First Event – Minister purportedly **told** state government officials that they could steal a little provide they were working hard.

Second Event – Minister *landed* the government in severe embarrassment after a video of him ***became*** public.

Example 07:

Taking a serious view of increasing incidents of attack on doctors and paramedical staff, government has ***promulgated*** an ordinance to make such incidents a cognizable offence.

Main verb – promulgated

-ING form of verb – taking

Explanation:

First Event – Government **took** a serious view of increasing incidents of attack on doctors and paramedical staff.

Second Event – Government has ***promulgated*** an ordinance to make such incidents a cognizable offence.

.

Example 08:

The SHO of concerned police station and the investigating officer have been *placed* under suspension, **taking** note of lapses in the investigation.

Main verb – placed

-ING form of verb – taking

Explanation:

First Event – Note of lapses in the investigation has been **taken**.

Second Event – The SHO of concerned police station and the investigating officer have been *placed* under suspension.

Example 09:

Long queues of vehicles are being *seen* on the highways **following** an alarming rise in the water level of the river.

Main verb – seen

-ING form of verb – following

Explanation:

First Event – There is an alarming rise in the water level of the river.

Second Event – Long queues of vehicles are being *seen* on the highways.

Example 10:

The court *found* him guilty of attempt to murder, **obstructing** and **assaulting** public servants and **injuring** the police officers to deter them from **performing** their duty.

Main verb – found

-ING form of verb – obstructing, assaulting, injuring, performing

Explanation:

First Event – He was accused of attempt to murder.

He was accused of **obstructing** public servants.

He was accused of **assaulting** public servants.

He was accused of **injuring** the police officers to deter them from **performing** their duty.

Second Event – The court *found* him guilty.

03 -- Using '-ING Form of Verbs' (III)

In the following examples, –ING form of verbs have been used to show 'Second Event' in the sentence.

Example 01:
Driver **overshot** the signal, **causing** the accident and **injuring** the hundreds.
Main verb – overshot
-ING form of verbs – causing, injuring
Explanation:
First Event – Driver **overshot** the signal.
Second Event – Driver **caused** the accident that **injured** the hundreds.

Example 02:
Heavy rain accompanied by thunderstorm *lashed* the city since Monday night, **breaking** all previous records of single day rainfall in the last 50 years for the month of February.
Main verb – lashed
-ING form of verb – breaking
Explanation:
First Event – Heavy rain accompanied by thunderstorm *lashed* the city since Monday night.
Second Event – Heavy rain **broke** all previous records of single day rainfall in the last 50 years for the month of February.

Example 03:
HC has *directed* the DGP to file a reply, **giving** details about the factories **manufacturing** illicit arm which have been unearthed in the last three years.
Main verb – directed
-ING form of verb – giving, manufacturing
Explanation:
First Event – HC has *directed* the DGP to file a reply.

Second Event – DGP has to **give** details about the factories which are **manufacturing** illicit arm.

These factories have been unearthed in the last three years.

Example 04:
Providing relief to the common man as well as to policymakers, softening food prices *pulled* down inflation to an over three-year-low.
Main verb – *pulled*
-ING form of verb – *providing*
Explanation:
First Event – Softening food prices *pulled* down inflation to an over three-year-low.

Second Event – It **provided** relief to the common man as well as to policymakers.

Example 05:
A Texas fertilizer factory *exploded* in a huge fireball, **flattening** nearby homes and **killing** as many as 15 people and **injuring** 160, with one official **likening** the blast to a "nuclear bomb".
Main verb – *exploded*
-ING form of verb – *flattening, killing, injuring, likening*
Explanation:
First Event – A Texas fertilizer factory *exploded* in a huge fireball.
Second Event – Explosion **flattened** nearby homes.
Explosion **killed** as many as 15 people.
Explosion **injured** 160 people too.
One official **likened** the blast to a "nuclear bomb".

Example 06:
He *punched* a man in the face and broke his nose before **going** on a rampage with hockey sticks, **swinging** at windows, lights, furniture and other items.

Main verb – punched

-ING form of verb – going, swinging

Explanation:

First Event – He **punched** a man in the face and broke his nose.

Second Event – He **went on** a rampage with hockey sticks.

He **swung** at windows, lights, furniture and other items.

Example 07:

Agriculture department **raised** the alarm over rampant use of pesticides in agriculture produce directly **affecting** the health of both soil and consumers.

Main verb – raised

-ING form of verb – affecting

Explanation:

First Event – Agriculture department **raised** the alarm over rampant use of pesticides in agriculture produce.

Second Event – Pesticides directly **affects** the health of both soil and consumers.

Example 08:

Everyone **plunged** into the lake, some **struggling** into life jackets, other **clinging** to flimsy paddle board.

Main verb – plunged

-ING form of verb – struggling, clinging

Explanation:

First Event – Everyone **plunged** into the lake.

Second Event – Some **struggled** into life jackets.

Other **clung** to flimsy paddle board.

Example 09:

Forces **busted** two militant hideouts **recovering** a huge arm cache.

Main verb – busted

-ING form of verb – recovering

First Event – Forces _busted_ two militant hideouts.

Second Event – Forces **recovered** a huge arm cache.

Example 10:

Roads were **laid** without digging out the earlier layer, **resulting** in roads being on higher than ground level.

Main verb – laid

-ING form of verb – resulting

Explanation:

First Event – Roads were **laid** without digging out the earlier layer,

Second Event – It **resulted** in roads being on higher than ground level.

Example 11:

Train _derailed_ **killing** 100 people and **trapping** some passengers in wreckage.

Main verb – derailed

-ING form of verb – killing, trapping

Explanation:

First Event – Train _derailed_.

Second Event – 100 people were **killed.**

Some passengers **trapped** in wreckage.

Example 12:

Two political leaders had _approached_ the session's court **challenging** the order of a magistrate, **saying** it would bar them from contesting the next elections.

Main verb – approached

-ING form of verb – challenging, saying

Explanation:

First Event – Two political leaders had _approached_ the session's court.

Second Event – They **challenged** the order of a magistrate.

They **said** it would bar them from contesting the next elections.

Example 13:

They **entered** the place **saying** that they have come for booking the place for a marriage because such functions take place there.

Main verb – entered

-ING form of verb – saying

Explanation:

First Event – They **entered** the place.

Second Event – They **said** that they had come for booking the place for a marriage.

They were under the impression that such functions are taken place there.

Example 14:

A 40-year-old businessman from India was **killed** by two unidentified gunmen, **leading** to scores of people of Indian origin in Nepal **sitting** on sit-ins outside a hospital **demanding** action from the Nepalese government against the attackers.

Main verb – killed

-ING form of verb – leading, sitting, demanding

Explanation:

First Event – A 40-year-old businessman from India was **killed** by two unidentified gunmen.

Second Event – This event **led** to scores of people of Indian origin in Nepal **sitting** on sit-ins outside a hospital.

They **demanded** action from the Nepalese government against the attackers.

Example 15:

Water **gushed** down **bringing** with it debris and boulders with unimaginable force **smashing** and **carrying** away everything.

Main verb – gushed

-ING form of verb – bringing, smashing, carrying
Explanation:
First Event – Water **gushed** down.
Second Event – Water **brought** with it debris and boulders with unimaginable force.
Water along with debris and boulders **smashed** and **carried** away everything.

Example 16:
Storm *hit* Canada's' largest city, **shutting** down subways, **forcing** some people to cling to trees and **leaving** about 1,400 passengers stranded for hours on a commuter train filled with gushing water.
Main verb – hit
-ING form of verb – shutting, forcing, leaving
Explanation:
First Event – Storm *hit* Canada's largest city.
Second Event – Subways were **shut** down.
Some people were **forced** to cling to trees.
About 1,400 passengers were **left** stranded for hours on a commuter train filled with gushing water.

Example 17:
The roof of the hotel *crashed* **resulting** in the building collapse **leaving** a dozen dead.
Main verb – crashed
-ING form of verb – resulting, leaving
Explanation:
First Event – The roof of the hotel *crashed*.
Second Event – Crash **resulted** in the building collapse.
Building collapse **left** a dozen dead.

Example 18:

Local residents *raised* slogans against the leader and *chased* him away; **forcing** him to flee on foot till his driver came to the spot and rescued him.

Main verbs – raised, chased

-ING form of verb – forcing

Explanation:

First Event – Local residents *raised* slogans against the leader and *chased* him away

Second Event – They **forced** him to flee on foot till his driver came to the spot and rescued him.

Example 19:

Fires in leftover vegetation from winter can easily get out of control and **spread** quickly, **putting** people, property and the environment at risk.

Main verb – spread

-ING form of verb – putting

Explanation:

First Event – Fires in leftover vegetation from winter can easily get out of control and **spread** quickly

Second Event – It can **put** people, property and the environment at risk.

Example 20:

The fire had **burnt** telephone and Internet cables in parts of the city **causing** a breakdown in communication in government offices and banks.

Main verb – burnt

-ING form of verb – causing

Explanation:

First Event – The fire had **burnt** telephone and Internet cables in parts of the city.

Second Event – The fire **caused** a breakdown in communication in government offices and banks.

Example 21:

The condition of road has **exacerbated** due to heavy rains in the city **making** it even more difficult for the commuters, who get stuck in big potholes and at times, are at risk of getting injured.

Main verb – exacerbated

-ING form of verb – making

Explanation:

First Event – The condition of road has **exacerbated** due to heavy rains in the city.

Second Event – The exacerbated condition has **made** the road even more difficult for the commuters.

Commuters, who get stuck in big potholes and at times, are at risk of getting injured.

Example 22:

Nepal was **devastated** by a 7.8 magnitude earthquake in 2015, **raising** alarm about the risks of flash flooding from glacial lakes.

Main verb – devastated

-ING form of verb – raising

Explanation:

First Event – The Nepal was devastated by a 7.8 magnitude earthquake in 2015.

Second Event – Earthquake **raised** alarm about the risks of flash flooding from glacial lakes.

Example 23:

Serpentine queues outside bill counters **reached** up to the main roads, **leading** to traffic congestion in many parts of the city.

Main verb – reached

-ING form of verb – leading

Explanation:

First Event – Serpentine queues outside bill counters **reached** up to the main roads in many parts of the city.

Second Event – These queues **led** to traffic congestion.

Example 24:

Chief executive officer _said_ that it was time for him to retire, **triggering** immediate speculation about his future plans.

Main verb – said

-ING form of verb – triggering

Explanation:

First Event – Chief executive officer _said_ that it was time for him to retire.

Second Event – His statement **triggered** immediate speculation about his future plans.

Example 25:

We unanimously _elected_ her as our leader **enabling** her to take over the reins from her predecessor.

Main verb – elected

-ING form of verb – enabling

Explanation:

First Event – We unanimously _elected_ her as our leader.

Second Event – Her election as our leader **enabled** her to take over the reins from her predecessor.

Example 26:

Water level of rivers _rose_ rapidly, **forcing** slum-dwellers living close to the river to move to safer place.

Main verb – rose

-ING form of verb – forcing

First Event – Water level of rivers *rose* rapidly.

Second Event – Slum-dwellers living close to the river were forced to move to safer place.

ADDITIONAL EXAMPLES:

Robert Mugabe *resigned* as Zimbabwe's president a week after the army and his former political allies moved against him, **ending** four decades of rule by a man who turned form independence hero to archetypal African strongman.

Toxic smoke emanating from the slowly burning garbage *created* a deadly smog **causing** problems for residents living nearby.

During the peak tourist season in the town, thousands of vehicles were *parked* at public places **causing** massive traffic jam and immense inconvenience to the public.

Both his legs were *afflicted* with polio when he was three, **leaving** him dependent on crutches to move around.

Major roads were *submerged* after about three hours of rains in the morning, **leading** to massive traffic jams in several areas.

04 -- Using 'With + -ING Form of Verbs'

Example 01:

Dengue crisis *continued* to rattle National Capital **with** a six-year-old boy and a woman **succumbing** to the vector borne disease, **raising** the toll to 11 *even as* the government **brought** a law to enable temporary takeover of private hospitals during emergencies.

Main verbs – continued, brought

-ING form of verbs – succumbing, raising

Explanation:

Dengue crisis *continued* to rattle National Capital.

A six-year-old boy and a woman **succumbed** to the vector borne disease.

This **raised** the toll to 11.

The government **brought** a law.

Law will enable temporary takeover of private hospitals during emergencies.

Example 02:

Our state will soon *launch* Metro rail project **with** the Centre **approving** state government's proposal for the mass transit system.

Main verb – launch

-ING form of verb – approving

Explanation:

Centre **approved** state government's proposal for the mass transit system.

Our state will soon *launch* Metro rail.

Example 03:

Project *rocked* both house of parliament **with** opposition **accusing** the government of attempting to destroy evidence of corruption.

Main verb – rocked

-ING form of verb – accusing

Explanation:

Project *rocked* both house of parliament.

Opposition **accused** the government of attempting to destroy evidence of corruption.

Example 04:
Session **began** on a stormy note **with** party **disrupting** the governor address, **forcing** him to leave.
Main verb – began
-ING form of verbs – disrupting, forcing
Explanation:
Session **began** on a stormy note.
Party **disrupted** the governor address.
Governor was **forced** to leave.

Example 05:
With heavy rainfall **lashing** various parts of city during the past 24 hours, water level in major rivers **continued** to rise, **putting** the authorities on alert.
Main verb – continued
-ING form of verbs – lashing, putting
Explanation:
Heavy rainfall **lashed** various parts of city during the past 24 hours.
Water level in major rivers **continued** to rise.
The authorities were **put** on alert.

Example 06:
The atmosphere **was** tense **with** many parents **choosing** not to take their children to school.
Main verb – was
-ING form of verb – choosing
Explanation:
The atmosphere **was** tense.
Many parents **chose** not to take their children to school.

Example 07:

River **was** extremely polluted **with** every kind of pollutant imaginable **including** toxins and carcinogens.

Main verb – was

-ING form of verb – including

Explanation:

River **was** extremely polluted.

There was every kind of pollutant imaginable.

Pollutant **included** even toxins and carcinogens.

Example 08:

He **said with** new delimitation **coming** into force, the purpose of creating the hill state would be **defeated**.

Main verbs – said, defeated

-ING form of verb – coming

Explanation:

He **said** new delimitation would be **coming** into force.

The purpose of creating the hill state would be **defeated**.

Example 09:

Rains **eased** power situation as the demand **dipped** sharply in the two states **with** minimum temperature in many parts **dropping** several notches below normal.

Main verbs – eased, dipped

-ING form of verb – dropping

Explanation:

Rains **eased** power situation.

The demand **dipped** sharply in the two states.

Minimum temperature in many parts **dropped** several notches below normal.

Example 10:

Alleged dubious land deals of CM *paralyzed* proceedings in Parliament on Tuesday, **with** the upper and lower house **witnessing** two adjournments **following** uproar by the opposition.

Main verb – paralyzed

-ING form of verbs – witnessing, following

Explanation:

Alleged dubious land deals of CM *paralyzed* proceedings in Parliament on Tuesday.

Opposition created uproar.

The upper and lower house **witnessed** two adjournments.

Example 11:

There *was* no respite from the scorching summer heat **with** the mercury **hovering** past 40 degree Celsius at many places.

Main verb – was

-ING form of verb – hovering

Explanation:

There *was* no respite from the scorching summer heat.

The mercury **hovered** past 40 degree Celsius at many places.

Example 12:

With the objective of **preventing** discharge of untreated industrial effluent and waste water into the river during the festival, officials have *shut* down as many as 75 tanneries in the city.

Main verb – shut

-ING form of verb – preventing

Explanation:

Officials have *shut* down as many as 75 tanneries in the city.

This has been done with an objective.

The objective has been to **prevent** discharge of untreated industrial effluent and waste water into the river during the festival.

Example 13:

The crisis in the ruling party *deepened* on Sunday **with** the rebel faction led by state party chief **setting** a July 12 deadline for **removing** CM and **replacing** him with his nominee.

Main verb – deepened

-ING form of verbs – setting, removing, replacing

Explanation:

The crisis in the ruling party *deepened* on Sunday.

The rebel faction led by state party chief **set** a July 12 deadline.

The rebel faction demanded for **removing** CM.

The rebel faction also demanded **replacing** him with his nominee.

Example 14:

With snags in power plants in the state **crippling** power supply, the state government has been *forced* to buy electricity worth dollar 1 million daily from the central pool.

Main verb – forced

-ING form of verb – crippling

Explanation:

Snags in power plants in the state **crippled** power supply.

The state government has been *forced* to buy electricity worth dollar 1 million daily from the central pool.

Example 15:

With the meteorological department **forecasting** heavy rainfall in the coming day and the rising floodwaters *entering* their houses, villagers are *forced* to move to higher ground, **leaving** behind their homes and other assets.

Main verb – forced

-ING form of verbs – forecasting, entering, leaving

Explanation:

The meteorological department has **forecasted** heavy rainfall in the coming day.

The rising floodwaters are **entering** into the houses of the villagers.

Villagers are **forced** to move to higher ground.

They are **leaving** behind their homes and other assets.

Example 16:

With the population of the city **touching** 2 million **and** an increment of 25,000 private vehicles every year, municipal authorities **are** yet to provide a parking facility to the city.

Main verb – are

-ING form of verb – touching

Explanation:

The population of the city has **touched** 2 million.

There is an increment of 25,000 private vehicles every year.

Municipal authorities **are** yet to provide a parking facility to the city.

Example 17:

With the two sides **sticking** to their positions, the likelihood of talks between them **appears** to be extremely remote.

Main verb – appears

-ING form of verb – sticking

Explanation:

The two sides have **stuck** to their positions.

The likelihood of talks between them **appears** to be extremely remote.

Example 18:

With the weather **fluctuating** between high temperatures during the day **and** drizzles at night, city hospitals are **seeing** an increase in cases of viral fever and respiratory illnesses **that** last more than a week.

Main verb – seeing

-ING form of verb – fluctuating

Explanation:

The weather is **fluctuating** between high temperatures during the day.

It drizzles at night.

City hospitals are *seeing* an increase in cases of viral fever and respiratory illnesses that last more than a week.

Example 19:

With Ebola cases *multiplying* with each passing day, government had *cancelled* the leaves of all doctors and paramedical staff including nurses and lab technicians.

Main verb – cancelled

-ING form of verb – multiplying

Explanation:

Ebola cases were **multiplying** with each passing day.

Government had **cancelled** the leaves of all doctors and paramedical staff.

Government had also **cancelled** the leaves of nurses and lab technicians.

Example 20:

With two sub-adult tigers **straying** into villages near the Tiger Reserve, the possibility of man-animal conflict has *increased* in the area.

Main verb – increased

-ING form of verb – straying

Explanation:

Two sub-adult tigers **strayed** into villages near the Tiger Reserve.

The possibility of man-animal conflict has *increased* in the area.

Example 21:

Opposition parties *attacked* external affairs minister for **helping** a fugitive in **getting** foreign travel documents, **with** many **demanding** minister's resignation and **dragging** PM into the raging row.

Main verb – attacked

-ING form of verbs – helping, getting, demanding, dragging

Explanation:

Opposition parties *attacked* external affairs minister.

She was said to have **helped** a fugitive in getting foreign travel documents.

Many **demanded** minister's resignation.

They also **dragged** PM into the raging row.

Example 22:

With tussle between Bar associations of the High Court and lower courts over pecuniary jurisdiction **resulting** in strikes by lawyers, the Apex Court *sought* response from both bodies on *why* they should not be charged with contempt for boycotting court proceedings in violation of its order.

Main verb – sought

-ING form of verb – resulting

Explanation:

Tussle between Bar associations of the High Court and lower courts over pecuniary jurisdiction **resulted** in strikes by lawyers.

The Supreme Court *sought* response from both bodies.

Both bodies were asked why they should not be charged with contempt for boycotting court proceedings in violation of its order.

Example 23:

With the rains not having fallen as they normally do, water levels *dropped* in a dam that supplies electricity to the country, **causing** power blackouts, business closures and consternation.

Main verb – dropped

-ING form of verb – causing

Explanation:

The rains have not been falling as they normally do.

Water levels *dropped* in a dam that supplies electricity to the country.

It **caused** power blackouts, business closures and consternation.

Example 24:

The air quality throughout the city has *improved* **with** the haze **abating** since last night due to increased rainfall.

Main verb – improved
-ING form of verb – abating
Explanation:
The air quality throughout the city has **improved**.
The haze has been **abating** since last night due to increased rainfall.

Example 25:
With the police **uncovering** a racket involved in killing camels for its meat and **seizing** four animals, two of them dead, from an old slaughterhouse in the city, cops **suspect** that this district has grown into a hub of camel slaughter over the years.
Main verb – suspect
-ING form of verb – uncovering, seizing
Explanation:
The police **uncovered** a racket involved in killing camels for its meat.
The police also **seized** four animals, two of them dead, from an old slaughterhouse in the city.
Now cops **suspect** that this district has grown into a hub of camel slaughter over the years.

Example 26:
All member banks of the association **joined** the nationwide strike, **with** the clerical staff not **providing** customer services.
Main verb – joined
-ING form of verb – providing
Explanation:
All member banks of the association **joined** the nationwide strike.
Clerical staff is not **providing** customer services.

Example 27:

Air travel is *set* to become a little more expensive **with** the government **proposing** 2% levy on all domestic and international tickets to raise funds for boosting regional air connectivity.

Main verb – set

-ING form of verb – proposing

Explanation:

Air travel is *set* to become a little more expensive.

The government **proposed** 2% levy on all domestic and international tickets to raise funds for boosting regional air connectivity.

Example 28:

The number of fatal accidents **seems** to be going up each year **with** the slew of campaigns being run on traffic rules and road safety guidelines **showing** very little or no impact whatsoever.

Main verb – seems

-ING form of verb – showing

Explanation:

The number of fatal accidents **seems** to be going up each year.

The slew of campaigns being run on traffic rules and road safety guidelines **showed** very little or no impact whatsoever.

Example 29:

With the natural water sources inside the park practically **drying up** due to the heat, officials have had to **arrange** for water tanks to ensure that the animals' drinking water requirements are adequately met.

Main verb – arrange

-ING form of verb – drying

Explanation:

The natural water sources inside the park practically **dried up** due to the heat.

Officials have had to **arrange** for water tanks to ensure that the animals' drinking water requirements are adequately met.

Example 30:

With entire state **sizzling** under a blistering heat-wave, the government which had earlier declared school holidays, till Tuesday, on Monday **announced** summer vacation in advance.

Main verb – announced

-ING form of verb – sizzling

Explanation:

Entire state is **sizzling** under a blistering heat-wave.

The government, on Monday **announced** summer vacation in advance.

The government had earlier declared school holidays, till Tuesday.

ALSO NOTE:

Use Of 'With' More Than One Times

Example:

With the state **suffering** one of the worst droughts in recent years **with** as many as 42 villages out of the 46 in the district already **declared** as affected by drought conditions **with** the total loss to standing crops **estimated** at dollar 3,000 million, the State Government has **sought** for Rs 1,000 million Central assistance as per the revised State Disaster Response Fund.

Explanation:

The state is **suffering** one of the worst droughts in recent years.

As many as 42 villages out of the 46 in the district are already **declared** as affected by drought conditions.

The total loss to standing crops is **estimated** at dollar 3,000 million.

The State Government has **sought** for Rs 1,000 million Central assistance as per the revised State Disaster Response Fund.

ADDITIONAL EXAMPLES:

Appalling conditions were **seen** in hospital **with** patients **lying** on the floor without food or water and almost no heating despite sub-zero temperatures at night.

Prospects of forming of an alliance between two parties for the upcoming polls **appeared** to have run into rough weather, **with** both parties today **hardening** their stance over sharing of seats.

Temperatures **dipped** across the state **with** several places **receiving** the first spell of winter rains.

With farmers not **turning up** at cold storage facilities to take away their potato produce, storage owners have **started** dumping the rotting tubers on roadsides for stray cattle to feed on.

The ruling party in the state **is** on the precipice of a split **with** party chief **expelling** chief mister and general secretary for six years after they summoned a party meet.

Several raids have been **conducted** in the highway, **with** officials **seizing** many overloaded vehicles.

With the water level in the rivers **rising** gradually, the state administration has **sounded** alert *asking* slum dwellers living close to the rivers to move to safer place.

With over 90 per cent of the crop **lost** due to untimely rains in the previous season, the farmers are now **looking** for alternative crops for survival.

Only the very best **participate** in prestigious Dubai Super Series Final tournament **with** only the top eight in the respective men's and women's singles ranking **earning** the right to compete.

A near total shutdown like situation **prevailed** in the city **with** shops and other establishments **downing** shutters and office goers **returning** home early as CM's health condition continued to remain critical.

With extreme weather events **increasing** in frequency there **is** crying need for much better coordination between meteorological department and state disaster management officials.

<u>05 -- Using 'Series'</u>

<u>Example 01:</u>
Culturally, ethnically, historically, linguistically, religiously, socially
there was no affinity whatsoever between Bengal and Darjeeling.
<u>Explanation:</u>
Culturally, there was no affinity whatsoever between Bengal and Darjeeling.
Ethnically, there was no affinity whatsoever between Bengal and Darjeeling.
Historically, there was no affinity whatsoever between Bengal and Darjeeling.
Linguistically, there was no affinity whatsoever between Bengal and Darjeeling.
Religiously, there was no affinity whatsoever between Bengal and Darjeeling.
Socially, there was no affinity whatsoever between Bengal and Darjeeling.

<u>Example 02:</u>
The *educational institutions, health centers, national highways, railway stations, stadiums* belong to us as much as they do to them.
<u>Explanation:</u>
The **educational institutions** belong to us as much as they do to them.
The **health centers** belong to us as much as they do to them.
The **national highways** belong to us as much as they do to them.
The **railway stations** belong to us as much as they do to them.
The **stadiums** belong to us as much as they do to them.

<u>Example 03:</u>
Residents are taking extra care that the disease does not spread, by buying *mosquito repellant sprays, creams, liquid vaporizer machines, coils, patches, band/bracelets, mosquito nets, electric racquets* of various brands.
<u>Explanation:</u>

Residents are taking extra care that the disease does not spread.

They are buying **mosquito repellant sprays** of various brands.

They are buying **creams** of various brands.

They are buying **liquid vaporizer machines** of various brands.

They are buying **coils** of various brands.

They are buying **patches** of various brands.

They are buying **band/bracelets** of various brands.

They are buying **mosquito nets** of various brands.

They are buying **electric racquets** of various brands.

Example 04:

The children will *swarm the streets, wave the National flag, sing patriotic songs* and *greet city residents* on Independence Day.

Explanation:

The children will **swarm the streets** on Independence Day.

They will **wave the National flag**.

They will **sing patriotic songs**.

They will **greet city residents**.

Example 05:

Unfortunately, the administration had played into rival's hands *by being imprecise, by being unprepared, by lacking focus, by being ad hoc, by not doing sufficient hard-nosed groundwork, good old-fashioned diplomacy and preparation.*

Explanation:

It is unfortunate that the administration had played into rival's hands.

Government **had been imprecise**.

Government **had been unprepared**.

Government **had lacked focus**.

Government **had been ad hoc**.

Government **had not done sufficient hard-nosed groundwork**.

Government **had not done good old-fashioned diplomacy**.

Government **had not done preparation**.

Example 06:

Funds were released for *conservation and preservation of heritage buildings, extension and digitalization of library for preservation of rare books, setting up of museum* and *starting diploma and certificate courses in heritage and cultural studies.*

Explanation:

Funds were released for **conservation and preservation of heritage buildings.**

Funds were released for **extension and digitalization of library for preservation of rare books.**

Funds were released for **setting up of museum.**

Funds were released for **starting diploma and certificate courses in heritage and cultural studies.**

Example 07:

Our city has huge potential for different forms of mountain biking on account of its diversity in the form of *rivers, valleys, waterfalls, rocky terrain, forests and meadows*, along with *snow-clad peaks* that offer unparalleled views.

Explanation:

Our city has huge potential for different forms of mountain biking.

It is on account of its diversity in the form of **rivers**.

It is on account of its diversity in the form of **valleys**.

It is on account of its diversity in the form of **waterfalls**.

It is on account of its diversity in the form of **rocky terrain**.

It is on account of its diversity in the form of **forests**.

It is on account of its diversity in the form of **meadows**.

It is on account of its diversity in the form of **snow-clad peaks** that offer unparalleled views.

Example 08:

He is *being educated, living a normal life, growing up healthily* and *does not wish to be disturbed*.

Explanation:

He is **being** educated.

He is **living** a normal life.

He is **growing** up healthily.

He **does not wish** to be disturbed.

Example 09:

Kindly do not post any *personal, abusive, defamatory, infringing, obscene, indecent, discriminatory* or *unlawful* or similar comments.

Explanation:

Kindly do not post any **personal** comments.

Kindly do not post any **abusive** comments.

Kindly do not post any **defamatory** comments.

Kindly do not post any **infringing** comments.

Kindly do not post any **obscene** comments.

Kindly do not post any **indecent** comments.

Kindly do not post any **discriminatory** comments.

Kindly do not post any **unlawful** comments.

Example 10:

There is more to road safety much beyond the emphasis on *using helmets, avoiding overspeeding, desisting from talking on mobile phone while driving,* and *avoiding drunk driving*.

Explanation:

There is more to road safety much beyond the emphasis on **using helmets**.

There is more to road safety much beyond the emphasis on **avoiding overspeeding**.

There is more to road safety much beyond the emphasis on **desisting from talking on mobile phone while driving**.

There is more to road safety much beyond the emphasis on **avoiding drunk driving**.

Example 11:
RTO enforcement teams are going to act tough against violations like *over speeding, jumping the red light, overloading goods carriage vehicles* and *two-wheelers being driven without helmets*.

Explanation:
RTO enforcement teams are going to act tough against the following violations:

Over speeding

Jumping the red light

Overloading goods carriage vehicles

Two-wheelers being driven without helmets

Example 12:
Ever wonder what celebrities would look like without all the *grooming, priming, styling* and *money*?

Explanation:
Ever wonder what celebrities would look like without **grooming**?
Ever wonder what celebrities would look like without **priming**?
Ever wonder what celebrities would look like without **styling**?
Ever wonder what celebrities would look like without **money**?

Example 13:
He was *racing down hills, chasing through fields* and *walking through the meadows* to school.

Explanation:
He was **racing down** hills.
He was **chasing through** fields.
He was **walking through** the meadows to school.

Example 14:

The format of the questions included *multiple choices, gap-fills, short answer questions, matching* and *true/false/not given.*

Explanation:

The format of the questions included **multiple choices.**

The format of the questions included **gap-fills.**

The format of the questions included **short answer questions.**

The format of the questions included **true/false/not given.**

Example 15:

Footage on local TV networks showed *smashed windows, blackened walls* and *smoke billowing out of the fortified villa.*

Explanation:

Footage on local TV networks showed **smashed windows.**

Footage on local TV networks showed **blackened walls.**

Footage on local TV networks showed **smoke billowing out of the fortified villa.**

Example 16:

They could die anytime, anywhere – *shot in a bus, blown upon a street, massacred in a market, bombed on a train.*

Explanation:

They could die anytime.

They could die anywhere.

They could be **shot in a bus.**

They could be **blown upon a street.**

They could be **massacred in a mark**et.

They could be **bombed on a train.**

Example 17:

The stadium saw it happen, *eyes wide open, hands in the air, hearts pounding, throats screaming in one huge roar.*

The people in the stadium saw it happen.

Their **eyes were wide open.**

Their **hands were in the air.**

Their **hearts were pounding.**

Their **throats were screaming in one huge roar.**

Example 18:

Boulders covered the ***mall patches of agricultural land, most livestock*** ***had perished, shops had been destroyed, roads had disappeared,*** ***power lines had snapped.***

Explanation:

Boulders covered the **mall patches of agricultural land.**

Most livestock had perished.

Shops had been destroyed.

Roads had disappeared.

Power lines had snapped.

Example 19:

The governor has the power to grant ***pardons, reprieves, respites*** or ***remissions*** of punishments or to ***suspend, remit or commute*** the sentence of any person convicted of any offence against any law.

Explanation:

The governor has the power to grant **pardons.**

The governor has the power to grant **reprieves.**

The governor has the power to grant **respites.**

The governor has the power to grant **remissions** of punishments.

The governor has the power to **suspend** the sentence.

The governor has the power to **remit** the sentence.

The governor has the power to **commute** the sentence.

The governor can use this power for any person convicted of any offence against any law.

Poles were erected, wires were strung, bulbs lit up, fans whirred and the village experienced its first "electric moment".

Explanation:

Poles were erected.

Wires were strung.

Bulbs lit up.

Fans whirred.

The village experienced its first "electric moment".

Example 21:

We express **_surprise, delight, admiration, sympathy or understanding_** according to the situation.

Explanation:

We express **surprise** according to the situation.

We express **delight** according to the situation.

We express **admiration** according to the situation.

We express **sympathy** according to the situation.

We express **understanding** according to the situation.

Example 22:

A dew-drenched lotus her seat, red silk her attire, gold her ornamentation, she was the very personification of auspiciousness.

Explanation:

She was the very personification of auspiciousness.

A dew-drenched lotus was her seat.

Red silk was her attire.

Gold was her ornamentation.

Example 23:

Country was plagued with *militancy, a near-failed economy, endemic corruption, chronic power cuts* and *crumbling infrastructure.*

Explanation:

Country was plagued with **militancy**.

Country was plagued with **a near-failed economy**.

Country was plagued with **endemic corruption**.

Country was plagued with **chronic power cuts**.

Country was plagued with **crumbling infrastructure** too.

Example 24:

Hundreds of thousands of people packed together, *dancing, singing, chanting, hawking*, and just *celebrating* each other's presence.

Explanation:

Hundreds of thousands of people packed together.

They were just **celebrating** each other's presence.

They were **dancing**.

They were **singing**.

They were **chanting**.

They were **hawking**.

Example 25:

They were *screaming, shouting, roaring, wailing and hooting*.

Explanation:

They were **screaming**.

They were **shouting**.

They were **roaring**.

They were **wailing**.

They were **hooting**.

Example 26:

They were *suffering silently, waiting patiently, praying fervently*.

Explanation:

They were **suffering silently**.

They were **waiting patiently**.

They were **praying fervently**.

Example 27:

Soul *directs, enlivens, galvanizes,* and *moves* the body, mind and senses.

Explanation:

Soul **directs** the body, mind and senses.

Soul **enlivens** the body, mind and senses.

Soul **galvanizes** the body, mind and senses.

Soul **moves** the body, mind and senses.

Example 28:

Seniors have assessed him as *competent, honest, hardworking, Intelligent* and *sincere.*

Explanation:

Seniors have assessed him as **competent.**

Seniors have assessed him as **honest.**

Seniors have assessed him as **hardworking.**

Seniors have assessed him as **Intelligent.**

Seniors have assessed him as **sincere.**

Example 29:

Rise above all *ethnic, linguistic, regional* and *sectarian* biases at the earliest.

Explanation:

Rise above all **ethnic** biases at the earliest.

Rise above all **linguistic** biases at the earliest.

Rise above all **regional** biases at the earliest.

Rise above all **sectarian** biases at the earliest.

Example 30:

Celebrations were marked with *great joy, gaiety, splendor* and *patriotic fervor.*

Explanation:

Celebrations were marked with **great joy**.

Celebrations were marked with **gaiety**.

Celebrations were marked with **splendor**.

Celebrations were marked with **patriotic fervor**.

Example 31:

We kept on *playing, roaming, singing, chatting* in our school trip.

Explanation:

We kept on **playing** in our school trip.

We kept on **roaming** in our school trip.

We kept on **singing** in our school trip.

We kept on **chatting** in our school trip.

Example 32:

They saw a donkey, *running, jumping* and *rolling* in the dust.

Explanation:

They saw a donkey.

Donkey was **running** in the dust.

Donkey was **jumping** in the dust.

Donkey was **rolling** in the dust.

Example 33:

He *owned, traded, bought, sold* or *hired out* buffaloes for his livelihood.

Explanation:

He **owned** buffaloes for his livelihood.

He **traded** buffaloes for his livelihood.

He **bought** buffaloes for his livelihood.

He **sold** buffaloes for his livelihood.

He **hired out** buffaloes for his livelihood.

<u>Example 34:</u>
The queen was loved and loathed in equal measure as *she crushed the unions, privatized vast swathes of industry, clashed with the other leaders* and *fought a war to recover the Islands from invaders.*

<u>Explanation:</u>
The queen was loved and loathed in equal measure.
She **crushed the unions**.
She **privatized vast swathes of industry**.
She **clashed with the other leaders**.
She **fought a war to recover the Islands from invaders**.

<u>Example 35:</u>
I *gathered strength, managed to cross the river, crossed to the other side* and *reached the empty building.*

<u>Explanation:</u>
I **gathered** strength.
I **managed** to cross the river.
I **crossed** to the other side.
I **reached** the empty building.

<u>Example 36:</u>
As news of the killing of a youth in police custody spread, hundreds of residents *attacked the police station, snatched rifles from policemen, indulged in brick-batting* and even *tried to set the police station on fire.*

<u>Explanation:</u>
News of the killing of a youth in police custody spread.
Hundreds of supporters *attacked the police station*.
They *snatched rifles from policemen*.
They *indulged in brick-batting*.
They *tried to set the police station on fire*.

Example 37:

While police asked the driver of the truck carrying 30 animals to stop, instead he *picked up more speed, rammed into a police barricade and finally collided with a roadside tree*.

Explanation:

Police asked the driver of the truck carrying 30 animals to stop.

Driver **picked up more speed.**

He **rammed into a police barricade.**

He finally **collided with a roadside tree.**

Example 38:

The **breakup** of the budgetary allocation is – *$400 million for Education, $300 million for Health, $250 million for Road Transport, $200 million for Agriculture, $150 million for Sanitation...*

Explanation:

The **breakup** of the budgetary allocation is as follows:

$400 million for Education

$300 million for Health

$250 million for Road Transport

$200 million for Agriculture

$150 million for Sanitation

Example 39:

Scam included *waiving police verification to recruit several with criminal records, forging examination papers and caste certificates, fudging scores* and *even changing laid-down criteria to favour candidates*.

Explanation:

Scam included **waiving police verification to recruit several with criminal records.**

Scam included **forging examination papers and caste certificates.**

Scam also included **fudging scores.**

Scam included even **changing laid-down criteria to favour candidates.**

Example 40:

Party president posed questions including *why so many MLAs failed to retain their seats, what were the party's shortcomings, did it put up the best possible candidates*.

Explanation:

Party president posed questions.

Questions included the following ones:

Why so many MLAs failed to retain their seats?

What were the party's shortcomings?

Did it put up the best possible candidates?

Example 41:

Democracy is the best system for *promoting moral behaviour, eradicating corruption, ensuring access to electricity and water,* and *providing people with healthcare.*

Explanation:

Democracy is the best system.

Democracy **promotes moral behaviour**.

Democracy **eradicates corruption**.

Democracy **ensures access to electricity and water**.

Democracy **provides people with healthcare**.

Example 42:

Infusing a sense of accountability among police through adequate legislative measures, insulating them from interference, abolition of orderly system, increasing representation of women in police, registration of FIRs using citizen-friendly technology and *setting up separate investigation and law and order wings in state police* were among the key recommendations of the ARC to be discussed in the meet.

Explanation:

The following were some key recommendations of the ARC to be discussed in the meet:

To Infuse a sense of accountability among police through adequate legislative measures

To insulate them from interference

Abolition of orderly system

To increase representation of women in police

Registration of FIRs using citizen-friendly technology

To set up separate investigation and law and order wings in state police

Example 43:

It is that time of the year when students are *gearing up for admissions, visiting counsellor, and planning further studies.*

Explanation:

It is that time of the year.

Students are *gearing up for admissions*.

Students are *visiting counsellors*.

Students are *planning further studies*.

Example 44:

The hostages - *head bowed, looking somber,* and *some fighting back tears, stood* behind the bar.

Explanation:

The hostages **stood** behind the bar.

Their **heads were bowed**.

They **looked somber**.

Some of them **fought back tears**.

Example 45:

Seeking to speed up development of the northeast, the National Advisory Council has favoured *internet connectivity to the region through*

Bangladesh, daily direct flights from each of the seven state capitals to Delhi and *a separated plan to implement healthcare initiatives.*

Explanation:

The National Advisory Council has **sought** to speed up development of the northeast.

It has favoured *internet connectivity to the region through Bangladesh*.

It has also favoured *daily direct flights from each of the seven state capitals to Delhi*.

It favoured *a separated plan to implement healthcare initiatives* too.

Example 46:

Thief was *slapped, punched* and *kicked* before *being pushed* out of the premises.

Explanation:

Thief was **slapped**.

Thief was **punched**.

Thief was **kicked**.

Thief was **pushed out** of the premises.

Example 47:

Combo schemes, free home delivery, huge discounts and *full refunds if the product is returned* are terms that online buyers would associate with *clothes, gizmos* and *other merchandize.*

Explanation:

Online buyers would associate the following terms with *clothes, gizmos* and *other merchandize:*

Combo schemes

Free home delivery

Huge discounts

Full refunds if the product is returned

Example 48:

A lot of hoopla was created, with *ribbons being cut, speeches made, concerts organized*, etc.

Explanation:

A lot of hoopla was created.

Ribbons were being cut.

Speeches were being made.

Concerts were being organized.

Example 49:

From six in the evening to 6 pm, he meets different sections of society including *local intellectuals, teachers, administrators, various activists' groups,* and *party units*.

Explanation:

From six in the morning to 6 pm, he meets different sections of society.

He meets **local intellectuals.**

He meets **teachers.**

He meets **administrators.**

He meets **various activists' groups.**

He meets **party units.**

Example 49:

Your housing costs include your *mortgage payments, property taxes, maintenance, cleaning, furniture* and *insurance.*

Explanation:

Your housing costs include your *mortgage payments.*

Your housing costs include your *property taxes.*

Your housing costs include your *maintenance.*

Your housing costs include your *cleaning.*

Your housing costs include your *furniture.*

Your housing costs include your *insurance.*

Example 50:

He **stood** up, **opened** his mouth, **stuck** his tongue out, **raised** his right arm and **shook** his forefinger angrily at him.

Explanation:

He **stood** up.

He **opened** his mouth.

He **stuck** his tongue out.

He **raised** his right arm.

He **shook** his forefinger angrily at him.

Example 51:

Taking electricity to all the villages by the end of the year, **reining** in migration from the hills through employment generations and **putting** an end to illegal mining and prevalent cheating of people in registry of land purchased by them are among the priorities of our government.

Explanation:

The priorities of our government are as follows:

To **take** electricity to all the villages by the end of the year

To **rein** in migration from the hills through employment generations

To **put** an end to illegal mining and prevalent cheating of people in registry of land purchased by them

ADDITIONAL EXAMPLES:

An university had come out with what students called "draconian rules" that forbid them from "any form of protest" such as **raising slogan, participating in hunger strikes, demonstration, sit-ins,** or **even talking to the media**.

Absence of parapets-crash barriers, over-crowding, untrained maneuvering at sharp turns, drunken driving, tiredness of drivers, poor maintenance of vehicles, and **driving while playing loud music** are the major factors behind road accidents in the hills.

According to medical science, insomnia (inability to sleep) alone affects 8-10% of the population and may lead to increased risk of **hypertension, diabetes milletus, headache, immune deficiency, anxiety, depression, memory problems, road traffic accidents** and **decreased work performance.**

At the turn of the century, India was home to more than 40,000 tigers but **shrinking of habitat, lack of proper food and shelter, increasing human intervention and encroachment** and **excessive poaching** pushed the species to the brink of extinction.

Birth defects can be the result of **genetics, life-style choices and behaviours of parents, exposure to certain medicines or chemicals, infections during pregnancy,** or a combination of these factors.

Difficult working conditions, low salary, slow promotion, lack of job security, no fixed hour of job, harsh rules for appointment, and **impounding of certificates** at the time of appointment were some of the problems faced by nursing staff.

First priority of any government should be to bring **the confidence, the energy, the enthusiasm, the trust** *in the minds of every citizen.*

We need to **track the terrorists, dismantle their networks, cut off their financing** and **stop propaganda** and radicalization.

Green Tribunal directed that no authority shall grant permission for construction of **building, houses, hotels** or **any structures** within 200 meters of shore of river at the highest food line without prior approval.

With **markets dimming, banks slipping into an area of darkness, exports melting,** and **consumer demand flickering,** our nation needs oxygen in the form of bold reforms and visionary policies.

CEOs forum identified six themes as important areas of collaboration to take forward – **smart cities and digital economy, healthcare, education and skills, engineering, defence and security,** and **financial and professional services.**

One in three Americans does not get enough sleep, leading to **obesity, diabetes, heart disease, mental illness** and **other chronic conditions,** health officials have warned.

We are **confidently, consistently** and **ceaselessly** working to integrate our economy with the world.

If you thought **price controls, compulsory exports, diktats to banks, quotas, surcharges,** and **prohibitive import duties** went out of fashion when we liberalized our economy two decades back, you need to think again.

She lived a wonderfully full life and was adored by her **family, friends, neighbours, acquaintances, colleagues,** and **the millions of fans** who she had been entertaining for over four decades.

Strike was believed to have affected the functioning of various essential services like **banking, power supply, oil and gas, transport, warehousing** and **other vital public services.**

The residents of our city used to have a flair for athletics whether it was **boxing, hockey, football, table tennis, badminton, sprinting** or any other sport.

New stadium will include a track for *800 meter race, a hockey field, badminton court, table tennis and lawn tennis, a boxing ring, a cricket and a football ground* and *swimming pool* along with other facilities.

The machine, which costs around dollar quarter a million dollars, allowed the company to create *curves, lines, intricate cuts* and *complex images*.

With more than 600 government and private hospital facilities of different categories in the region, including *district level hospitals, primary health centers, community health centers, state allopathic hospitals, two base hospitals* and *one government medical college*, this division generates more than 150 kg biomedical waste each day.

Whether you like it or not, you are being judged every day by the people you work with, be it *your colleagues, managers, clients* or *stakeholders.*

Do you know how much you should get paid on the basis of your *skill set, previous work experience, education* and *age?*

Whoever in any public place or in any other place within public view *burns, mutilates, tramples, defaces, defiles, disfigures, destroys, tramples upon* or otherwise shows disrespect to or brings into contempt (whether by words, either spoken or written, or by acts) the National Flag, may be punished with imprisonment for a term which may extend for three years, or with fine, or with both.

Too much sugar can be detrimental to *health, rotting teeth, building fat, damaging blood vessels* and *stressing out the system that regulates blood sugar.*

Are you able to *check your blood sugar, take medications or treat low blood sugar*, anywhere and at any time?

Can you figure out what is wrong with a young woman who develops *nausea, vomiting, weakness and confusion after weight-loss surgery*?

Most job seekers stress over *resumes, cover letters, potential interview questions* and *wardrobe*.

Temblor *reduced houses to rubble, brought down a local market* in a nearby community and *left streetlights* and *debris scattered* helter-skelter.

We wander over landscapes, whether *terrestrial, cosmic or conceptual,* looking for something *different, better, more interesting*.

It has become a fast developing town with *flats, apartments, houses, offices and shopping malls* coming up with amazing briskness.

Papers related to the *national building code, omission of firms name under public private partnership, no objection certificate from the fire department* and *others* were some of key papers that were allegedly missing from the file that were sent to education board for further process.

Prime Minister put national capital on maximum security alert, *shutting the* Metro, *postponing* football matches and *waning* citizens to avoid *shopping centers, airports, rail stations* and *concerts* because of a "serious and imminent" threat of *coordinated, multiple Iraq-style* terror attacks.

Autonomous colleges frame their *own syllabus, set question papers and conduct their own examinations, decide their own admission policies, have complete freedom to appoint its own administrative and academic staff* and *fix fees* for its academic programmes.

The judge slapped varying amounts of fines on the convicts after finding them guilty on various charges, including *hatching a criminal conspiracy to carry out the blasts, waging war against the nation, supplying arms and ammunition,* and *other serious offences.*

Issues related to *migration, bio-economy, climate change, ecosystem service, green house, disaster risk reduction* and *green technology* were discussed in a two-day Himalayan Sustainable Development Summit.

He has received odd injuries including *multiple fractures, head injuries, broken ribs, ligaments* and *dislocated shoulders* after a car tumbled down crushing him between metal sheets.

Tree-felling in mountainous topography sets off *landslides, soil erosion, running off rain water,* and *depletion of ground water.*

Weather forecast of thunder showers, warnings for heavy rain throwing normal life out of gear, water woes, electricity breakdown, road blocks, landslides, floods, disruption of provisional supplies and *other accompanying miseries,* don't act as deterrents for rain lovers.

Illegal parking of vehicles on the roadside, mushrooming of unauthorized multi-storied building apartment without basic amenities, unbridled encroachment on every nook and corner, open stinky drains, pot-holes, dusty and narrow roads, parking of unauthorized vehicles and *congestion on every road due to heavy traffic,* have made living in many cities a nightmare.

Can the bill pass all-party scrutiny today, *be introduced* in the Lower House, *get passed* there, then *be introduced* in the Upper House and *get passed* there in a grand total of five days.

The president of the country called the display of military prowess *"unbelievable," "amazing," "incredible," "brilliant"* and *"genius"*.

Many accidents could be attributed to human errors, but *faulty road design, absence of street lights, lack of dividers,* and *potholes on roads* also contribute to such incidents.

He had been found dead with his *throat slit, head battered* and *stab marks all over the body.*

All religions teach us that *care, compassion, concern, dedication, devotion* and *love* are important.

The forensic labs are consulted for testing of *hand writing, signature matching, digital data recovery, tampering of digital data, blood related tests* and *chemical toxins*.

Waste overflowing on roads, flies hovering over heaps of rubbish, and stray animals wandering around has become a common sight on many roads these days.

Apart from helping you think more clearly and calmly, meditation can help you *express yourself better, boost creativity, make you more observant, revitalize your mind, encourage you to let go of negative feelings* and *evoke feelings of gratitude*.

<u>06</u> -- Using 'From – To'

Example 1:
From school kids **to** college graduates **to** office goers **to** house-makers, everyone needs learning English.

Explanation:
School kids **need** learning English.
College graduates **need** learning English.
Office goers **need** learning English.
House-makers **need** learning English.

Example 2:
He enquired **from** the accident of Justin **to** the exit of Vera **to** poor security.

Explanation:
He **enquired** the *accident* of Justin.
He **enquired** *exit* of Vera.
He **enquired** *poor security*.

Example 3:
From the nib of a pen **to** shoes, zip of the trouser **to** coil of iron – the smugglers were using all these things to hide gold.

Explanation:
The smugglers were **using** *nib* of a pen to hide gold.
They were **using** *shoes* to hide gold.
They were **using** *zip* of the trouser to hide gold.
They were **using** *coil* of iron to hide gold.
They were using all these things to hide gold.

Example 4:
From gender **to** race **to** income, which cities worldwide are most equal?

Explanation:
Which cities worldwide are most **equal** in terms of gender?

Which cities worldwide are most **equal** in terms of race?

Which cities worldwide are most **equal** in terms of income?

Example 5:

From mobile phones **to** cricket gloves, **from** notebooks, scissors, and multiple-choice answer sheets **to** guns – everything is designed for the convenience of right-handed people.

Explanation:

Mobile phones are **designed** for the convenience of right-handed people.

Cricket gloves are **designed** for the convenience of right-handed people.

Notebooks are **designed** for the convenience of right-handed people.

Scissors are **designed** for the convenience of right-handed people.

Multiple-choice answer sheets are **designed** for the convenience of right-handed people.

Guns are **designed** for the convenience of right-handed people.

Everything is **designed** for the convenience of right-handed people.

Example 6:

From the district magistrate **to** the superintendent of police, the chief development officer **to** the chief medical officer, **from** the village council president **to** the sub-divisional magistrate, it is the ladies who had grabbed almost every top administrative post in the district.

Explanation:

Post of district magistrate had been **grabbed** by a lady in the district.

Post of superintendent of police had also been **grabbed** by a lady in the district.

Post of chief development officer had also been **grabbed** by a lady in the district.

Post of chief medical officer had also been **grabbed** by a lady in the district.

Post of village council president had also been **grabbed** by a lady in the district.

Post of sub-divisional magistrate had also been **grabbed** by a lady in the district.

Almost every top administrative post had been **grabbed** by ladies in the district.

Example 7:

Many ex-prisoners struggle **from** being introduced to modern technology, **to** navigating public transportation, **to** opening a bank account, **to** making simple life choices like what to buy at the grocery store.

Explanation:

Many ex-prisoners **struggle** to get introduced to modern technology,

They **struggle** to navigate public transportation.

They also **struggle** to open a bank account.

They even **struggle** to make simple life choices like what to buy at the grocery store.

Example 8:

Tax rates on over 200 items, ranging **from** chewing gum **to** chocolates, **to** beauty products, wigs and wrist watches, have been cut to provide relief to consumers and businesses.

Explanation:

Tax rates on over 200 items have been cut to provide relief to consumers and businesses.

These items include chewing gum, chocolates, beauty products, wigs and wrist watches.

ADDITIONAL EXAMPLE

From growing divorce cases of parents **to** dysfunctional families **to** a changing atmosphere in educational institutions, children are increasingly finding it difficult to cope with situations.

07 -- Using 'Connecting Words or Phrases'

01. ALONGSIDE
Example:
He *held* out the verification form *that* had a police stamp *alongside* another unrelated document stamped by the police.
Explanation:
He *held* out the verification form that had a police stamp.
He also held out another unrelated document stamped by the police.

02. AFTER
Example:
Fifteen wagons of a goods train *caught* fire between ABC and XYZ railway stations *after* some bogies *derailed* in the wee hours on Friday morning, *throwing* rail traffic out of gear on the National-State Capital route.
Explanation:
Some bogies *derailed* in the wee hours on Friday morning.
Fifteen wagons of a goods train *caught* fire between ABC and XYZ railway stations.
Rail traffic was *thrown* out of gear on the National-State Capital route.

Additional Examples:
Twelve primary school teachers in the district have been sacked by the basic education officer **after** it was found the certificates submitted by them for procuring their jobs were fake.

Long tailbacks were witnessed in gridlocked roads due to severe water-logging on National highway **after** heavy rains lashed the city leaving thousands of commuters stranded and forcing authorities to clamp prohibitory orders.

03. APART FROM

Example:

Apart from *ordering* the government to ban tobacco products, the court had also *asked* the government to submit a compliance report, *giving* details of the steps it had taken to implement the court's directives.

Explanation:

The court had *ordered* the government to ban tobacco products.

The court had also *asked* the government to submit a compliance report.

Government was asked to *give* details of the steps it had taken to implement the court's directives.

04 (A). AS

Example:

Cyclone *weakened* on Thursday afternoon into a tropical storm, *causing* far less damage than had been feared **as** it *passed* over coastal Bangladesh and *spared* Myanmar almost entirely.

Explanation:

Cyclone *weakened* on Thursday afternoon into a tropical storm.

Cyclone *caused* far less damage than had been feared.

Cyclone *passed* over coastal Bangladesh.

Cyclone *spared* Myanmar almost entirely.

Example:

All services, including *air travel, telephony, eating out and banking* became expensive **as** the government decided to impose a 0.5% cess on all taxable services to fund the space programme.

Explanation:

All services, including *air travel, telephony, eating out and banking* became expensive.

It happened because the government decided to impose a 0.5% cess on all taxable services to fund the space programme.

Example:
Many villages are inhabited only by those over 60 years old **as** their children have moved out in search of better jobs and opportunities.

Explanation:
Many villages are inhabited only by those over 60 years old.
Villagers' children have moved out in search of better jobs and opportunities.

Additional Examples:
Students from public schools have access to coaching classes and better study material unlike government school students **as** most of them come from financially constrained backgrounds.

She couldn't stop his eyes from welling up with tears **as** she saw her son in an Army officer's uniform at the Military Academy's passing out parade.

Thousands of people were stranded in the port areas **as** airlines cancelled flights and ferries were prevented from sailing.

04 (B). AS + AFTER

Example:
Authorities *lifted* curfew from all affected parts of the country *as* no major accident of violence was *reported* for two days *after* the protest *turned* violent early this week.

Explanation:
The protest had *turned* violent early this week.
No major accident of violence was *reported* for two days.
Authorities *lifted* curfew from all affected parts of the country.

04 (C). AS + THEREBY

The residents of the village finally heaved a sigh of relief **as** two had pumps were installed in their area **thereby** providing a solution to the water crisis in their areas.

04 (D). AS + THOUGH

Example:

Though the roads *are* wide in many areas, commuters are *left* with little space *as* vehicles are *parked* on roadsides, and shopkeepers have *encroached* the remaining part of roads.

Explanation:

The roads *are* wide in many areas.

Vehicles are *parked* on roadsides.

Shopkeepers have *encroached* the remaining part of roads.

Commuters are *left* with little space

04 (E). AS WELL AS

The lungs of children living in the cities with the highest pollution do not function **as well as** those of children living in rural areas.

There has been a rush among students **as well as** researchers to apply for patents.

04 (F). AS + WHERE/WHOM

He sat in the doctor's office, *where* he had come to get some medication for his fourteen year old son; *whom* he thought was suffering a mild depressive episode *as* a result of the change from elementary school to junior high school.

Explanation:

He sat in the doctor's office.

He had come there to get some medication for his fourteen year old son.

His son was suffering a mild depressive episode.

Depressive episode was a result of the change from elementary school to junior high school.

05. BEFORE

Example:

The authenticity of his complaint would be investigated **before** a first inspection report is lodged.

06 (A). BESIDES

Example:

In a move to discipline errant drivers, the road transport ministry favoured steep fines and imprisonment **besides** suspension or cancellation of driving license for serious traffic offences.

Explanation:

The road transport ministry favoured suspension or cancellation of driving license for serious traffic offences.

The road transport ministry also favoured steep fines and imprisonment to discipline errant drivers for serious traffic offences.

Example:

Plastic spoons and thermocol plates and cups are a big health hazard **besides** being dangerous for the environment.

06 (B). BESIDES + AFTER

A regional airline terminated services of two of its ground staff **besides** suspending three more employees at the airport for a week **after** investigations found multiple security breaches by a high-ranking security official at the aerodrome.

Explanation:

Investigations found multiple security breaches by a high-ranking security official at the aerodrome.

On the basis of investigations, a regional airline terminated services of two of its ground staff.

Airline also suspended three more employees at the airport for a week.

07. BUT

Example:

I remember feeling rather fearful when I first arrived at his home, **but** as the evening progressed my anxiety melted away and I relaxed.

Example:

I have been thinking about changing jobs for a while now **but** most of the placement agencies have told me to stay put.

08. DEPEND ON

Example:

They will *register* a case ***depending on*** what comes out in the fire department inquiry.

Explanation:

It **depends on** what comes out in the fire department inquiry.

Then only they will *register* a case.

09. DESPITE

Example:

The government auditor is *understood* to have raised questions over various aspects of the chopper deal, *including* conduct of trials outside the country ***despite*** the defence ministry *rejecting* such a proposal twice.

Explanation:

The government auditor is *understood* to have raised questions over various aspects of the chopper deal.

Deal *included* conduct of trials outside the country.

The defence ministry had *rejected* such a proposal twice.

Example:

Pro-democracy demonstrators approached the court for help as the government remained unperturbed **despite** all their attempts to draw attention to their cause through non-violent measures like hunger strikes and fasts unto death.

Explanation:

Pro-democracy demonstrators approached the court for help as the government remained unperturbed.

They had made all their attempts to draw attention to their cause.

They had taken resort to non-violent measures like hunger strikes and fasts unto death.

10. DUE TO

Example:

Government has *initiated* the process of closure of around 300 private schools running without recognition in the national capital **due to** their failure to meet the minimum land requirement and quality standards prescribed under the Right to Education Act.

Explanation:

Government has *initiated* the process of closure of around 300 private schools running without recognition in the national capital.

They failed to meet the minimum land requirement and quality standards prescribed under the Right to Education Act.

Example:

A mini-bus was hit by a train at an unmanned railway crossing this morning **due to** alleged negligence of the bus driver who ignored warning.

Explanation:
A mini-bus was hit by a train at an unmanned railway crossing this morning. The bus driver was negligent and ignored warning.

Additional Examples:
A majority of farmers had to sell their paddy produce to private traders **due to** a disorganized government paddy procurement system.

For the last 15 years he was suffering with a severe pain in his shoulders and knees **due to which** he could not do his daily chores such as having bath, and could not even sleep.

11. EVEN AS
Example:
Widespread rain *continued* on Saturday in north France, *bringing* temperatures down **even as** the water-logging *created* major inconvenience across region.
Explanation:
Widespread rain *continued* on Saturday in north France.
Continuous rain *brought* temperatures down.
Water-logging *created* major inconvenience across region.

12. FOLLOWING
Example:
Life is gradually limping back to normalcy after the weather stabilized **following** ten days of heavy incessant rain that had brought life to a standstill.

13. IN ADDITION

Example:

In addition to the Navy's probe, two parallel investigations were *progressing* - one by Delhi Police, and another by Mumbai Police.

Explanation:

Two parallel investigations were *progressing*.

One was progressing by Delhi Police.

Another was progressing by Mumbai Police.

These probes were being done *in addition* to the Navy's probe.

14. INSTEAD OF

Instead of just increasing revenue by installing water meters, authorities should focus on providing clean water to the public.

Explanation:

Authorities should focus on providing clean water to the public.

It is not good to just increase revenue by installing water meters.

15. IN CASE

Example:

In case he *fails* to make the payment within the specified time, a recovery certificate will be *issued* against him and the officers will be *asked* to collect the money.

Explanation:

He may *fail* to make the payment within the specified time.

In this situation, a recovery certificate will be *issued* against him.

Officers will be *asked* to collect the money.

16. ONLY TO BE

Example:

They were *sent* on Tuesday for their first posting **only to be** *handed over* termination letters on Wednesday.

Explanation:

They were *sent* on Tuesday for their first posting.

They were *handed over* termination letters on Wednesday.

17 (A). THAT

Examples:

The army and the air force have now been kept on standby to join firefighting operation **that** already have 3 companies of *National Disaster Response Force, police, NGOs and the general public* trying to tackle the inferno.

The bridge that villagers built by tying wooden plans together was so flimsy **that** the river current washed it away in a few days.

17 (B). AND + THAT

Example:

Members of a particular community had *filed* a couple of petitions *challenging* the high court ruling **and** *lined* up a bevy of senior advocates to advance arguments to convince the Supreme court **that** the constitutionally guaranteed right to profess a religion of one's choice included practicing its *tenets, traditions and customs.*

Explanation:

Members of a particular community had *filed* a couple of petitions.

They had *challenged* the high court ruling.

They had *lined* up a bevy of senior advocates to advance arguments to convince the Supreme Court.

Their argument was that the constitutionally guaranteed right to profess a religion of one's choice included practicing its *tenets, traditions and customs.*

17 (C). SO THAT

Example:

To combat man-animal conflict, an NGO started distributing gas stoves, LPG cylinders and related equipment in the vicinity of Tiger Reserve **so that** people living in nearby villages do not have to go trespass into the forest to collect fuel.

18. SUBSEQUENTLY

Example:

The state government had earlier announced closure of schools, both government-run and private ones, till April 25 and **subsequently** decided to extend the school holidays till April 30 in view of the weather condition.

Explanation:

The state government had earlier announced closure of schools, both government-run and private ones, till April 25.

The state government decided to extend the school holidays till April 30 in view of the weather condition.

19 (A). THOUGH

Example:

We have been fighting our battle for a long time **though** it has not reached any conclusion till now.

19 (B). EVEN THOUGH

Example:

There has been no rain for the past four months, **so** all sources of water have dried up, **even though** there are taps in front of everyone's house.

20. UNLIKE

Example:

He has been working at the same post and drawing the same salary for 30 years, **unlike** colleagues who were at his level, who have been promoted.

Explanation:

He has been working at the same post and drawing the same salary for 30 years.

His colleagues, who were at his level, have been promoted.

21. WHERE

Example:

His car veered onto the opposite lane of the highway, **where** it was hit by a truck coming down from the opposite direction.

22. WHERE

Example:

Navy ships and aircraft had been searching since the afternoon **when** a chartered plane lost contact with air traffic controllers.

23. WHICH

Example:

The leopards were *counted* using the same methods adopted for the tiger census, **which** involved *getting* pictures of animals through camera-trapping **and** *gathering* other evidence of their presence, **and** then *extrapolating* the numbers to over the entire forest landscape.

Explanation:

The leopards were *counted* using the same methods adopted for the tiger census.

Methods involved *getting* pictures of animals through camera-trapping.

Methods also involved *gathering* other evidence of their presence.

Methods then involved *extrapolating* the numbers to over the entire forest landscape.

Example:
Employees were protesting against the administration **which** had failed to construct the houses **that** were promised to them three years ago.

Explanation:
Employees were protesting against the administration.
Administration had failed to construct the houses.
Houses were promised to them three years ago.

Additional Examples:
There is urgent need to improve infrastructure in our village – **which** has been witnessing a steady spate of migration.

It appeared he had concealed information pertinent to his case, **which** he ought to have disclosed when he had filed the petition in the court.

Unqualified men are being posted on key positions, **which** is extremely dangerous and a big threat for the country.

Drains are often choked by trash thrown on the road **which** leads to dirty water flowing on the streets.

People park their vehicles on roadsides **which** in turn add to the chaotic traffic scene in the city.

Rare wild animal skins and parts were being smuggled, **after which** forest officers had set up a team to nab the culprits.

For long, he has had a reputation for speaking his mind, **by which** people usually mean speaking what is on their minds.

They were warned for trespassing into forest land by pitching tents, **for which** they could neither show the permission letter nor give any satisfactory Explanation:.

24. WHILE
Examples:
Banks met with limited success to handle the huge pay-day rush, **while** ATMs continued to remain mostly dry, causing hardship to people.

Ten injured were taken by ambulance to hospital **while** four others made their own way to hospitals.

25. WITH
Example 01:
This figure has *earned* India the third rank among the top 10 countries *with* the highest number of globally threatened bird species.
Explanation:
This figure has *earned* India the third rank among the top 10 countries.
India has very high number of globally threatened bird species.

Example 02:
Transportation of foodstuff by road to far-flung area has taken a hit, *with* the network of major roads and highways still damaged.
Explanation:
Transportation of foodstuff by road to far-flung area has taken a hit.
The network of major roads and highways is still **damaged**.

Example 03:

The tradition of oral learning has been a hallmark of Indian culture, **with** ancient scriptures and epics **passed** on orally for generations.

Explanation:

The tradition of oral learning has been a hallmark of Indian culture. Ancient scriptures and epics **passed** on orally for generations.

Example 04:

There are around 1000 primary and upper primary government schools across the district, **with** a majority of them **situated** in remote areas and without proper amenities.

Explanation:

There are around 1000 primary and upper primary government schools across the district

A majority of them **situated** in remote areas and without proper amenities.

Example 05:

With incidents of violence being regularly reported from the college, the district administration **has served** notice to 10 trouble-mongers that includes 7 students and five outsiders.

Explanation:

Incidents of violence are being regularly reported from the college,

The district administration **has served** notice to 10 trouble-mongers that includes 7 students and five outsiders.

Example 06:

With the number of tractor-trolleys carrying bricks increasing in the city, the question of safety of people **has risen.**

Explanation:

The number of tractor-trolleys carrying bricks are increasing in the city.

The question of safety of people **has risen.**

Example 07:

Bursting of crackers during New Year **had increased** the pollution level in various parts of the country, **with** toxic fumes from fireworks raising the particulate matter content in the air to five-seven times higher than the permissible limit.

Explanation:

Bursting of crackers during New Year **had increased** the pollution level in various parts of the country, Toxic fumes from fireworks raised the particulate matter content in the air to five-seven times higher than the permissible limit.

Example 08:

With so many rituals and things to do, the wedding day **turns** out to be the most chaotic day for almost every bride and groom.

Explanation:

The wedding day **turns** out to be the most chaotic day for almost every bride and groom.

There are so many rituals and things to do on wedding day.

Example 09:

Race *was* against time *with* only two days to go for the party to wrap up its session *and* one day less for CM to meet PM.

Explanation:

Race *was* against time.

There were only two days to go for the party to wrap up its session.

There was one day less for CM to meet PM.

Example 10:

The government agreed to provide 646 acres to TML on a 90-year lease on an annual rent of $1 million for the first five years and *with* an increase at the rate of 25 percent every five years *till* 30 years and after 30 years, the rent will be fixed at $5 million a year *with* an increase at the rate of 30 percent after every 10 years **till** the 60th year then the rent will be $20 million a year.

Explanation:

The government agreed to provide 646 acres to TML.

The government agreed to provide it on a 90-year lease.

An annual rent of $1 million for the first five years was fixed.

Rent will increase at the rate of 25 percent every five years till 30 years.

After 30 years, the rent will be fixed at $5 million a year.

Rent will increase at the rate of 30 percent after every 10 years

It will be so till the 60th year.

Finally the rent will be $20 million a year.

Additional Examples:

Days are windy and cool and there is moisture in air, **with** humidity above 80% in the past few days.

Hundreds of troops **established** a permanent presence in the disputed areas, **with** the construction of helipads, upgraded roads, pre-fabricated huts, shelters and stores to withstand the freezing winter.

The head post office in the city **is** reeling under staff crunch **with** only one-fourth of the sanctioned work force available on a given day.

08 – Using 'Parenthesis'

Parenthesis is a word, phrase or sentence that is added to a speech or piece of writing, with a view to provide extra information. Dashes, commas or brackets are used to separate parenthesis from the rest of the text.

Parenthesis (Dashes)
Example 1:
And the letter – *it could not be confirmed who it was addressed to* – said that "this is being done to make you pay for your sins."
Explanation:
It could not be confirmed who the letter was addressed to.
The letter said that "this is being done to make you pay for your sins."

Example 2:
One of the most potent weapons created to tackle the menace and bring the offenders to book – *the income tax department's directorate of criminal investigation* – stands dismantled and powerless.
Explanation:
The income tax department's directorate of criminal investigation is one of the most potent weapons.
It was created to tackle the menace and bring the offenders to book.
But it stands dismantled and powerless.

Example 3:
Which artists – *whether musicians, actors, writers, dancers, visual artists or some combination thereof* – would you like to see team up?
Explanation:
Which artists would you like to see team up?
Would it be musicians, actors, writers, dancers, visual artists or some combination thereof?

Example 4:

Many readers – *and I am one of them* – are fascinated by books written on English language skills.

Explanation:

Many readers are fascinated by books written on English language skills.
I am one of those fascinated readers.

Example 5:

The days of physical marketing – *flyers, billboards, posters, handouts* – are giving way to a new era of avant-garde media.

Explanation:

The days of physical marketing are giving way to a new era of avant-garde media.
Physical marketing includes flyers, billboards, posters, and handouts.

Example 6:

A face-off was building up between two Constitution bodies – *state assembly and the state information commission* – over the issue of jurisdiction.

Explanation:

A face-off was building up between two Constitution bodies over the issue of jurisdiction.
Those Constitution bodies were state assembly and the state information commission.

Example 7:

If there are complaints against officials and that too for a long period – *there were complaints against him in 2011; in 2014, many queries have revealed the same* – then if investigating agency probes, why is anyone so baffled?

Explanation:

If there are complaints against officials and that too for a long period then if investigating agency probes, why is anyone so baffled?

There were complaints against officials in 2011; in 2014, many queries have revealed the same.

Example 8:
Jurists were divided on whether she – *against whose acquittal in a disproportion asset case the Supreme Court is likely to deliver its verdict next week* – can be sworn-in.

Explanation:
Jurists were divided on whether she can be sworn-in.

The Supreme Court is likely to deliver its verdict next week against her acquittal in a disproportion asset case

ADDITIONAL EXAMPLES:
Changes in the environment – *reportedly largely due to greenhouse gases released into the atmosphere by human activity* – threaten to make earth uninhabitable for humans.

Canola oil – *one of the most widely consumed vegetable oils in the world* – may be harmful for the brain.

No one – *no matter what position he is sitting in* – should be allowed to do any unconstitutional work.

His salary – *to the tune of dollar 10,500* – was blocked by his employer without offering him any valid reason.

"No government servant shall – *in any radio broadcast, telecast through any electronic media or in any document published in his own name or anonymously, pseudonymously or in the name of any other person in any communication to the press or in any public utterance* – make any statement of fact or opinion *which* has the effect of an adverse criticism of any current or recent policy or action of the central government of state government," reads the service rules.

Parenthesis (Commas)

Example 1:
Guidelines issued in 2002, *in possession of national daily*, don't differentiate between officers and air warriors.
Explanation:
Guidelines issued in 2002.
Guidelines are in possession of national daily.
Guidelines don't differentiate between officers and air warriors.

Example 2:
The four, *all said to be cooks*, had tried to make special dinner.
Explanation:
The four had tried to make special dinner.
They all were said to be cooks.

Example 3:
A robbery attempt was failed when a girl, *whose room the robber tried to break into*, raised an alarm.
Explanation:
A robbery attempt was failed.
The robber tried to break into girl's room.
The girl raised an alarm.

Example 4:
The accused, *through his counsel*, has said in his petition that he is innocent.
Explanation:
The accused has said in his petition that he is innocent.
The accused said this through his counsel.

Example 5:

The central government has allowed its employees, *irrespective of their grade or post,* to fly on a vacation with family at its cost.

Explanation:

The central government has allowed its employees to fly on a vacation with family at its cost.

The central government has allowed this irrespective of employees' grade or post.

Example 6:

He did this, *with this person,* and did that, *with that person,* seemed to be the flavour of the season.

Explanation:

He did this, with this person.

He did that, with that person.

It seemed to be the flavour of the season.

Example 7:

A 30-year-old man, *whose last name indicated his Asian descent,* had been found dead at a university, alongside weapons and backpack of bombs, suggesting that he was plotting an attack.

Explanation:

A 30-year-old man had been found dead.

His last name indicated his Asian descent.

He had been found dead at a university.

He had been found alongside weapons and backpack of bombs.

It suggested that he was plotting an attack.

Example 8:

Rainwater, *which a leaking roof had deposited in various corners of the classroom*, collected in puddles or broke in to tiny streams, making its way dangerously close to the mats on the hard floor.

Explanation:

A leaking roof had deposited rainwater in various corners of the classroom.

Rainwater collected in puddles or broke in to tiny streams.

It made its way dangerously close to the mats on the hard floor.

Example 9:

Smoke from fireworks, *coupled with moisture and nearly stagnant wind movement,* shrouded the city in a thick cover of smog **with** respirable pollutants reaching perilous levels.

Explanation:

Smoke from fireworks shrouded the city in a thick cover of smog.

There was already moisture and nearly stagnant wind movement,

Respirable pollutants reached perilous levels.

Example 10:

He, *known for his clean image in the party,* is considered to be a strong hand in the organization.

Explanation:

He is known for his clean image in the party.

He is considered to be a strong hand in the organization.

ADDITIONAL EXAMPLES:

Jonathan, *once a successful businessman running five fabrication factories,* was forced to drive an auto-rickshaw after his business bust.

A child, *who was playing while her parents were busy in the wedding proceedings,* somehow managed to come out of the venue and lost his way back.

09 – Miscellaneous Patterns

(A). Using Past and Present Participle Forms of Verbs

Example:
Describing the two parties along with their allies *as* two sides of the same coin, he *emphasized* the need for transforming the political system **established** by these political parties.

Explanation:
He **emphasized** the need for transforming the political system.

He **described** the two parties along with their allies *as* two sides of the same coin.

That system was **established** by these political parties.

(B). Using 'One, Two, Three....'

Example 01:
He said he would like to be in the military camp but, '**One**, I am too old to be out there; **two**, I may not adjust with my colleagues; and **three**, my rivals would notice me'.

Explanation:
He said he would like to be in the military camp.

However, he regretted he could not be there for certain reasons.

He said, "I am too old to be out there."

He also said, "I may not adjust with my colleagues."

He further added, "My rivals would notice me."

A long sentence using 'Dash (-)', 'Series', 'Connecting Word', and '-Ing form of Verb':

A very severe cyclonic storm – *the most intense to have hit the country in two decades – **claimed** ten lives, **flattened** homes, **snapped** power,* communication lines and *threw* into disarray rail, road and air traffic *as* it crossed the coast *pounding* many cites with heavy rain and squall.

*Connecting Word – **as***
Part of sentence within dashes -- the most intense to have hit the country in two decades
*Verbs used to form series – **claimed, flattened, snapped, threw***
*-Ing form of Verb – **pounding***

<u>Try</u> <u>To</u> <u>Understand</u> <u>The</u> <u>Following</u> <u>Long</u> <u>Sentence:</u>

If it *appears* to the court that a victim *committing* suicide was hypersensitive to ordinary *petulance, discord and differences* in domestic life quite common to the society to *which* the victim belonged *and* such *petulance, discord and differences* were not expected to induce a similarly circumstanced individual in a given society to commit suicide, the conscience of the court should not be *satisfied* for *basing* a finding that the accused charged of *abetting* the offence of suicide should be *found* guilty.

****

About the Author

Manik Joshi, the author of this book was born on **Jan 26, 1979** at Ranikhet and is permanent resident of Haldwani, Kumaon zone of India. He is an Internet Marketer by profession. He is interested in domaining (business of buying and selling domain names), web designing (creating websites), and various online jobs (including 'self-publishing'). He is science graduate with ZBC (zoology, botany, and chemistry) subjects. He is also an MBA (with specialization in marketing). He has done three diploma courses in computer too. **ManikJoshi.com** is the personal website of the author.

Amazon Author Page of Manik Joshi:
https://www.amazon.com/author/manikjoshi

Email:
mail@manikjoshi.com

****

BIBLIOGRAPHY

'ENGLISH DAILY USE' TITLES BY MANIK JOSHI

01. How to Start a Sentence
02. English Interrogative Sentences
03. English Imperative Sentences
04. Negative Forms in English
05. Learn English Exclamations
06. English Causative Sentences
07. English Conditional Sentences
08. Creating Long Sentences in English
09. How to Use Numbers in Conversation
10. Making Comparisons in English
11. Examples of English Correlatives
12. Interchange of Active and Passive Voice
13. Repetition of Words
14. Remarks in English Language
15. Using Tenses in English
16. English Grammar- Am, Is, Are, Was, Were
17. English Grammar- Do, Does, Did
18. English Grammar- Have, Has, Had
19. English Grammar- Be and Have
20. English Modal Auxiliary Verbs
21. Direct and Indirect Speech
22. Get- Popular English Verb
23. Ending Sentences with Prepositions
24. Popular Sentences in English
25. Common English Sentences
26. Daily Use English Sentences
27. Speak English Sentences Everyday
28. Popular English Idioms and Phrases
29. Common English Phrases
30. Daily English- Important Notes

'ENGLISH WORD POWER' TITLES BY MANIK JOSHI

01. Dictionary of English Synonyms
02. Dictionary of English Antonyms
03. Homonyms, Homophones and Homographs
04. Dictionary of English Capitonyms
05. Dictionary of Prefixes and Suffixes
06. Dictionary of Combining Forms
07. Dictionary of Literary Words
08. Dictionary of Old-fashioned Words
09. Dictionary of Humorous Words
10. Compound Words in English
11. Dictionary of Informal Words
12. Dictionary of Category Words
13. Dictionary of One-word Substitution
14. Hypernyms and Hyponyms
15. Holonyms and Meronyms
16. Oronym Words in English
17. Dictionary of Root Words
18. Dictionary of English Idioms
19. Dictionary of Phrasal Verbs
20. Dictionary of Difficult Words

OTHER TITLES BY MANIK

01. English Word Exercises (Part 1)
02. English Word Exercises (Part 2)
03. English Word Exercises (Part 3)
04. English Sentence Exercises
05. Test Your English
06. Match the Two Parts of the Words
07. Letter-Order In Words
08. Simple, Compound, Complex, & Compound-Complex Sentences
09. Transitional Words and Phrases
10. Regular and Irregular Verbs

****

Made in the USA
Middletown, DE
16 February 2019